1120

D0987474

WE WANT TO LIVE

248.24

ROBERT CROSSLEY

We want to LIVE

INTER-VARSITY PRESS

INTER-VARSITY PRESS
Inter-Varsity Fellowship
39 Bedford Square, London WC1B 3EY

© INTER-VARSITY PRESS
First Edition, May 1967
Reprinted, January 1968
Reprinted, May 1972

ISBN 0 85110 338 3

Biblical quotations are from the Revised
Standard Version unless otherwise stated

Printed in Great Britain by
Hazell Watson & Viney Limited
Aylesbury, Bucks

Contents

Contents

1 Purpose

曾老長 敎督基華中城多入拿加
CHINESE PRESBYTERIAN CHURCH
177 Beverley St. at Baldwin
Toronto 2B, Ontario, Canada

No-one, so far as I know, asked to be born; very few indeed have any say at all about the home or the family in which they are brought up. So when we arrive at an age when we want to start sorting out life for ourselves, we are apt to find to our frustration that much of the sorting out has been done already, and that without our conscious knowledge or consent. Like a ship, our initial design and building will largely determine our capabilities, and our launching will, at least to begin with, determine our direction of travel.

By the time we reach college or university or embark on a career, therefore, two things have happened. First, we have reached the age of wanting to run our own life in our own individual way; and second, we have just been through a process which makes this difficult – perhaps even impossible. No wonder, then, that there is often a feeling of frustration and a strong desire to break all past ties and be free.

Of course, it is important to think clearly about this desire to be free. It has both a negative and a positive side. On the one hand, we long to be free from all restraints. This is perhaps natural, but largely negative. On the other, we want to shape our own life, and, above all, to be ourselves. This is healthy and positive, but far from easy to achieve. Too often, it merely turns into a blind desire to follow the 'fashion', whether it be the fashion in clothes, literature or morals. This is not freedom at all, and to be moulded by our contemporaries will not necessarily produce a better result than to be moulded by our elders!

Sometimes the desire for freedom will take the form of wanting to get married as soon as possible. This seems to combine the relief of breaking with authority and restraint with the positive ideal of shaping our own life. But it is relevant to ask whether our ideal really does stop short at turning into one more white-collar worker in one more suburban home, or one more housewife coping with one more set of children. Some dream of money, rather than marriage, as their way to freedom (those who achieve both are few and far between!), but are we sure that we want to turn into one more surtaxed director tied to one more city desk, and probably a stomach ulcer into the bargain?

For the more courageous, the age-old means of cutting loose was to go off in search of adventure, perhaps to become famous as an explorer. But there is not much of the world left to explore nowadays, and it is, perhaps, a sad reflection on the modern world that the director, the scientist, and even the artist, all look depressingly similar, whether they happen to be in the Arctic, the Azores, or in Ascot. As someone said many years ago: 'There is nothing new under the sun.'

We are, in any case, assuming that we will have a

future in which to work out our purpose in living. Many people are frustrated and depressed today not merely because they find it hard to be themselves as true individuals, but because on top of that time seems to be short. Who can say how many more years of peace this country can expect to enjoy? Have you ever asked yourself what the odds are against your ever reaching old age? There was a time when war was glamorous and could itself be a means of self-expression and adventure. There must be few who think like that today. The probability is that there would be nothing left to express.

These are probably some at least of the thoughts, ideas and longings which jostle each other in your mind in your more thoughtful moments. What makes this a serious matter is that there is a real possibility that they will go on jostling about in your mind, without ever really resolving themselves, until your dying day – whenever that may be.

Is it, in fact, possible to live a meaningful life today? Equally important, is it possible to take all that has gone before in your life and turn it to good account as you seek to become a real individual with a real and complete personality?

What has been said already about marriage and office jobs is a pointer to the fact that man's search for self-fulfilment tends to focus on two main points: sex (in its broadest meaning) and career. Let us look at these a little more closely.

Sex lies at the very basis of personality and is undoubtedly one of the major driving forces in life. But is it capable on its own of bringing either meaning or fulfilment to one's life? Most people tend to think of sex as bringing a peculiarly individual flavour to their lives, but this can very easily get out of proportion and become an illusion. T. S. Eliot stated only some thirty years ago that 'individualistic democracy has come to a high tide : and it is more difficult today to be an individual than it ever was before';[1] but he has also pertinently asked why it is that man thinks he is being most individual just when he is being most like everyone else. 'Violent physical passions', he once wrote, 'do not in themselves differentiate men from each other, but rather tend to reduce them to the same state.'[2] Nevertheless, sex seems to offer something slightly mysterious and exciting which can give expression and meaning to life. Sex has been recently described as the 'mysticism of materialism' and as the only possible religion for a materialistic society. But is this not to claim for it far more than it is, in point of fact, capable of being? Mysticism can prove curiously elusive; it is the sort of thing which tends to slip right from under your fingers. You make a grab at the rainbow and wonder why you are left with nothing more exciting than a handful of air. Like a mirage, mysticism can look like the answer to many problems from a sufficient distance, but if you stake everything on it as a life-saver, you are likely to end up even less satisfied than before. A religion – mystical though it may be – must be able to do better than that.

The second focal point through which we seek to find meaning and purpose in living is our career. The best qualifications will mean the best and most interesting

[1] From *Faith that Illuminates*, 1935.
[2] From *After Strange Gods*, 1934.

job with the best salary. Not only will this enable us to give expression to our capabilities, and to spend most of our time doing something which we find reasonably interesting; it will also enable us to earn enough money to acquire at least some of the good things of life which clamour for our attention from every advertisement and shop window, each claiming an indispensable place in any full life.

A career may take many forms, but there are two fields in particular which seem to offer special opportunities for self-expression and which beckon with special appeal to those on the search for 'truth' in life : one is the arts and the other is science.

The arts cover a wide field, including the four main streams of painting, music, literature and drama. These can, of course, be combined in many ways, and there is often a subtle blending of sex which appeals in a special way because here seems to be the ideal combination of the mystical and the practical. For those with sufficient talent it is possible to make a very successful career out of the arts, although the demands of technique mean that the 'mystical' has to give a good deal of ground to the severely 'practical'. But the basic aim is to express yourself and the world in objective terms and thereby seek to penetrate to the meaning of life itself.

The arts are, indeed, a means of self-expression which can bring much satisfaction and fulfilment, but it is as well to be clear in one's mind that there is no guarantee that you will know any more about the meaning of life at the end than you did at the beginning. To be honest, the search is not always quite genuine anyway. It does not take long to discover that the mystery and excitement last only so long as nothing is clarified. You have to keep the edges blurred and your feet well off the ground. You want to discover the meaning of life, and yet you are a little frightened of actually doing so, in case it might prove too ordinary. So everything is kept in a state of suspended meaninglessness. You say you want simple truth, but everything is kept perpetually deep and complex. You are a seeker, but you are not too keen to find; the result might be too disturbing.

The other main field which seems to offer special rewards for those in search of meaning and truth in life is the sciences. The scope here is wide indeed, but the general method is the same. By precise observation and experiment we seek to discover the exact nature of ourselves and the world we live in, and so to penetrate to the heart of the meaning of life. The method is exciting and rewarding because, although it requires unlimited discipline and patience, it has yielded spectacular results in the past and will continue to do so, no doubt, in the future.

Of course, as with the arts, the picture tends to look more exciting from a distance than it does in close-up. Science is highly specialized and departmentalized, and you are hardly likely to discover the whole meaning of the universe on your own. You are more likely to spend your life in one tiny branch of industry or research, and (as with the arts) there is no guarantee that you will know any more about the meaning of life at the end than you did at the beginning. The crucial question remains : Will this kind of career, *on its own*, provide a real and adequate purpose in living ?

What particular combination of business, sex, arts and science you actually pursue will depend mainly on your background, your talents and your temperament. In the event, your choice is fairly limited. What is important to realize is that each of these categories shares two common features.

First, each is important and can play an essential part in any life. But second, when any one of them is pursued *for its own sake*, it turns out to be unsatisfactory. The road suddenly becomes a cul-de-sac. To fall into this trap is sometimes described as 'worshipping idols'. It is to treat the means as if they were an end, to pin one's faith on something which ultimately will not bear the weight. It is to worship a false god.

We have only one life and everyone wants to make the most of it. It must be a terrible experience to reach the end of one's life and then realize that it has been spent in pursuit of the wrong objective, that the road really has not led anywhere after all. Perhaps you get an inkling of it even now when you suddenly realize that time has passed, that opportunities have gone for ever, and that nothing worth-while has been achieved. It is a frightening experience.

Curiously, it is death which makes life seem so very important and profound. If we were all going to live for ever, then what we did with our time would not seem to matter so much. Certainly there would be no poetry, no great music or art. If there were no death, there would be no depth, no urgency about life, no profound sense of value and beauty such as that which made Walter de la Mare exhort us to 'look thy last on all things lovely, every hour'. It is death which ultimately forces us to face the question: What is the purpose of life?

How important it is then, at the outset of our career,

to think carefully about our life and what we want to do with it. How important to make sure that we are not being launched in a direction which is none of our choosing, that we are not chasing a mirage, that our dreams and ambitions will bear the weight of a lifetime, and that we are not treading the well-worn path to disillusionment and despair.

Like a child first learning to use his eyes, we have to learn to see in perspective, to understand what is important and what is only secondary. And how few people ever learn to tell the difference ! We must understand what things really matter, and what things do not ultimately matter at all.

This perspective is all important. If the right things are put first, then everything else has a habit of falling into place, almost as if by magic. And it is worth noting at this point that it was said long ago : 'Set your mind on God's kingdom and his justice before everything else, and all the rest will come to you as well.'[1]

Such a perspective and sense of value is essential if we are to find real purpose in life. It is essential if we are to find our true and satisfying place in the giant twentieth-century automated machine. It is essential if we are to be truly ourselves. But it requires an effort, it requires thought and it requires faith. If you do not stop and stand back and take a long look at yourself and the world while you have the chance, you will only too quickly be swept out on the tide and submerged in the mainstream of life. It is only those who have a clear idea of where they are going who have any chance of reaching their objective.

[1] Matthew 6:33, New English Bible.

The average student leaves school or university and goes into a branch of industry, private business or one of the professions. He will gradually progress over the years: he will learn his job and his salary will increase. By the time he is twenty-five or so he will marry and perhaps rent a flat or begin to buy a house. In due course he will have a family, move to another house and perhaps get another job or a better position. Many people, perhaps most, spend their whole lives in one job. He will see his children grow up, and he will see himself and his wife grow older. Eventually he will retire and perhaps move to the country. In all too short a time he will die – and then what? What has been the purpose of it all? What has it all meant in the end?

2 Value

The purpose and meaning of your life can really only be questions of any significance if we assume that your life is in some way valuable. If you are just one out of millions whose life is not in the least important one way or the other, then there is little point in talking about purpose in life; life has no purpose. It is a very different matter, however, if, as a man whom people cannot seem to forget taught years ago, even the hairs of your head are all numbered.

But what is the value of a human life and how are we to assess it? We instinctively feel ourselves to be valuable without necessarily being able to pin down just why this should be so. If you were put up for sale as a material object, all that would be visible to a purchaser is a complex collection of chemicals and water worth only a few shillings. If your physical and mental abilities were taken into account, the price would no doubt rise considerably, but this sale price would reveal your value only in terms of usefulness to other people, in other words as a slave – a basis of valuation recognized long ago as quite inadequate for a human personality.

Of course, there is a sense in which we put ourselves up for sale every time we apply for a job, but virtually the only time nowadays that the whole value of human life has to be assessed in money terms is when there is a case of compensation – for example, to a widow, following the accidental death at work of her husband. It is perhaps sobering to wonder just how much we would be worth in such a case. But even here such compensation can really be based only on potential earning power, and the real value of that human life cannot be fully expressed in money terms at all, as no doubt the widow would tell you.

Is there any other way, then, in which we can assess value apart from money? A way opens up when we recognize that money is worth nothing in itself; it is only a medium of exchange. It is, in fact, a convenient means of bartering. For example, I may see in a shop a beautiful antique piece of furniture which I value very highly. Unfortunately its price, which I consider reasonable, is £200, and I have no money. So I decide to sell my car for £200 and use the money to buy the furniture. The money has only been the medium of exchange. It does not represent any intrinsic value. I have shown my valuation of the piece of furniture in terms of my car and I consider that I have made a good bargain. Furthermore, I would not have been willing to make the exchange unless I wanted the furniture *more* than the car; in other words, I have made a profit in *real* (although of course not in money) terms.

We should notice in passing that this underlines the personal nature of value. The antique dealer's price represented his opinion of the value; the price I actually paid represented mine. A professional valuer could have helped me by examining the piece in detail and giving me comparative market prices and his own opinion. But he could not have decided the valuation for me. That piece of furniture may be worth *to me* either much more or much less than the average market price. A child passing the shop would probably not be prepared to exchange his ice-cream for that particular antique; that is his valuation. I was prepared to sell my car, and I show my own personal valuation by actually making the bargain and carrying out the transaction.

But to revert from furniture to people, we can begin to see here a basis for assessing how we value our own lives. Quite apart from what other people may think about us (and we must consider this in the next chapter), we show our valuation of ourselves quite clearly by *what we are willing to accept in exchange for our lives*.

I can explain and amplify this best by asking you to consider two very searching questions which Jesus Christ once asked his followers. In their context,[1] they read like this : 'If any man would come after me, let him deny himself and take up his cross and follow me. For whoever would save his life will lose it; and whoever loses his life for my sake and the gospel's will save it. For what does it profit a man, to gain the whole world and forfeit his life? For what can a man give in return for his life?'

We can leave aside for the time being the deeper

[1] Mark 8:34–37.

question of what he meant by the cross, and indeed we do not even need to assume the existence of God at this stage. You are simply asked, first, for what you would be willing to exchange your life; and then, second, you are invited to consider whether such an exchange would be a good bargain – whether in fact it would involve a profit or a loss. If a man spends his life becoming supremely successful in the world's eyes, but thereby loses his own soul, has he made a good bargain? Is his valuation of himself a high one or a low one?

We have seen already that value is a personal thing, which we must assess for ourselves, and we have to make up our own minds how we value our own lives. Other people can help us in our decision, but only we can make the actual exchange for ourselves. What is more, we *are* selling (or *spending*) our lives every day – we are trading them in a day at a time, and not often do we watch very carefully the exchange rate.

Our valuation of ourselves shows up in a hundred different ways, some very important, some apparently quite insignificant. If we lie, we exchange personal integrity for a possible temporary gain. If we wrongly indulge in sexual relations, we can exchange love for passing satisfaction (a marriage can be sold that way too). We can exchange an exam pass for a certain number of hours of laziness. We can exchange our health for a certain quantity of cigarettes or drugs. In a car we can exchange our lives for a certain amount of drink or a moment's recklessness. All these must surely be regarded by any thinking person as bad deals, exchanges which result in each case in a crippling loss.

There are some exchanges which we find less easy to assess. What about the business tycoon who makes a great fortune and lives in luxury, but as a result is hardly ever at home with his family, and has bad health and a short temper, and dies of a coronary about fifteen or twenty years before he need have done? Was it worth it? What about the undetected criminal who lives well on the proceeds of his theft, but can never have an easy mind about it? Or perhaps he has an entirely easy mind, in which case he would appear to have exchanged his conscience and power of discerning good from evil for the enjoyment of material things. In the long run, was it worth it?

Because we are spiritual as well as animal beings, we do not judge value by material standards alone. If we did, it would make the task of deciding value comparatively easy – the wealthiest and most successful man would always be the one who made the best out of life. But we know that this is not necessarily true. Real success is far more than just a material matter. What a person *is* proves to be more important (more valuable) than what he *has*, however difficult this may be to face up to in a world which tends to regard material things as all-important. Yet we manage to see other people in a better perspective than we see ourselves, and find ourselves making assessments which show our capacity for right valuation. We look, perhaps, at a rich businessman who seems to have everything (he may even think that he has), but who is nevertheless a bundle of nerves – constantly worrying, exploding and flapping. We cannot avoid the feeling that he is somehow a failure as a human being: that he gained materially only by the loss of something more important. On the other hand, we cannot help being challenged and sometimes severely shaken by those uncanny people who can give away everything (sometimes even their lives) without seeming to lose anything that matters.

What puts the edge on the whole matter, as we began to see in the first chapter, is the fact that we have only one life. In business, a bad valuation which results in a financial loss can sometimes be recouped the following year. But when it is our own lives that we are concerned with, there is the frightening possibility of reaching the end and realizing then that the years have been traded in and that there is little if anything of real value to show in exchange. Worst of all, by then it will be too late to do anything about it.

Only too easily we find ourselves in practice valuing our lives much too cheaply, exchanging the precious days and weeks for little or nothing. Deep down we know instinctively that we are worth more than this. But how are we to realize our true value? How are we to trade in our lives to the maximum advantage? In the quotation we have been considering, the speaker leaves us in no doubt as to his answer: 'If any man would come after me, let him deny himself and take up his cross and follow me. For whoever would save his life will lose it; and whoever loses his life for my sake and the gospel's will save it.'

The main force of this is clear enough. Jesus Christ is saying that to commit our lives to following him may appear to be a very bad bargain indeed, but it is the only way to realize our true value. To give our lives to be his disciples may look like throwing them away, but those who do so discover that it is an exchange which shows the very maximum of profit.

This is, of course, a matter which we must pursue further later on, but it is important here to realize that the majority of people seriously undervalue themselves; they exchange their lives for little or nothing. Probably, if you are honest with yourself, you are doing so too. The challenge of Jesus Christ to us to take his way might just have more in it than you suppose. It is worth very careful investigation. Nobody in their right senses wants to fritter away a valuable asset – especially when it happens to be a human life.

In the meantime, there is another aspect of value which we must consider. In our more sober moments we place a high value on our own lives – we would hardly be human if we did not. But supposing that our lives are, in fact, worth more even than we suppose? We must investigate this in the next chapter.

3 Love

In the last chapter, the discussion centred on our valuation of ourselves and the way in which this value can be realized. But there is another side to this altogether; to value ourselves is one thing, but to be valued by someone else is quite another. The acid test of our worth is the valuation placed upon us by other people. This is why love is so supremely important to us. We want, more than anything else, to be valued – and valued for our own sake, not for what we have. This is, incidentally, why love and sex can never be quite the same thing. You can indulge in sexual relations without being valued either by your partner or yourself. To be loved is quite different. It is to discover (to your immense surprise) that someone else places a tremendous value on you, a kind of value you never suspected you had and which honestly you do not feel you deserve.

The first love which most people experience is the love of their parents. A child, of course, would not normally put it in so many words, but he knows instinctively that he is somehow important and valuable. He knows that while he is at home, and even if he is naughty, he is somehow secure. If he ever begins to suspect that this is not true, the results can be disastrous. Everyone knows the close relationship between crime and broken homes. The person who is not loved feels lonely, lost and unimportant and this can express itself in many violent and anti-social ways.

Of course, the response of a child to his parents' love is variable and sometimes disappointing. Good parents will willingly give a home, education, protection and money to their child without looking for too much by way of direct return. It is certainly a mistake for parents to impress upon their child the idea that he owes them something. As I mentioned before, you did not ask to be born, nor is it entirely your fault if you have caused a lot of trouble and expense. But good parents hope that their child will show, not gratitude, but *love*, and their greatest reward should be to see their son or daughter growing up into a complete, mature personality in body, mind and spirit.

Eventually there should ideally come a time when this strong link of love with the parents is taken over by the love of a husband or wife. This does not mean, of course, that you suddenly cease to be loved by your parents, but your life becomes re-orientated away from them, and away even from yourself, towards your partner. It is your partner who gives you value and the sense of security and stability which you need. Such love can be the supreme experience in life because it proves to you beyond all shadow of doubt that you are indeed valuable and important.

Now what I have described is an ideal experience, which, if it was experienced ideally, might just possibly be adequate for your life. Even then it would actually break down at a number of points, of which perhaps the most important is that it would do nothing to answer the problem of the first chapter – what is the *purpose* of your life? In fact, the kind of love I have described is never experienced ideally, and a little thought will show that it can only really be the outward and human expression of something much deeper and ultimately more important. If human love were the ultimate criterion of value, then the child of an unhappy home, or the partner in an unsuccessful marriage, would always be less valuable and less important than the child who is loved or the happily married man and woman. Similarly the married man would always be more valuable than the bachelor and the child who has parents would be more valuable than the orphan.

This is clearly not true to human experience and it merely underlines the fact that human love is not an ultimately satisfactory basis for giving value to a person's life, because it is much too arbitrary and unstable. You can put a house on the market and discover that one day it is worth £10,000 and the next day it is worth virtually nothing, because the bottom has fallen out of the market. It may even be that you never find this kind of high market price at all, yet you know deep down that you are very far from valueless. Certainly if we base our whole lives on human love, we are building on a very uncertain foundation.

Yet love remains a supreme human experience because it is that which gives us the assurance that we are valuable. But how can we gain this love-value? Certainly we cannot pursue love, any more than we can pursue happiness, as we have already seen. To chase after value is to make sure that we never find it. We cannot make someone love us – we cannot place this kind of value upon ourselves.

But supposing just for a moment that it really is true that *God* loves you. This is, after all, the basic message of Christianity, and it merits the most serious consideration, even if in the end you cannot accept it. Certainly, if it is true, then it does make sense of all the questions raised so far.

In the first place, if God really loves you, it means that you can be sure beyond all doubt that you are of infinite value and importance. We have seen how value is measured by price, and if Christianity is true, then God has shown us beyond all possibility of misunderstanding that he was prepared to pay the very highest possible price for us – he was willing to die for us. How this could be is beyond our scope at this point, but the clear implication of Christ's death on the cross is that we are more valuable and important than we ever dreamed possible – that we have a value, in fact, which is potentially of an eternal quality. 'God so *loved* the world that he gave his only Son, that whoever believes in him should not perish but have eternal life.'[1]

If we are as valuable as this, then clearly it will make all the difference to the way we value our own lives and the way we trade them in. No-one would sell his house cheaply if he knew that there was a purchaser waiting at a price beyond his highest hopes.

Furthermore, not only would the love of God for you be constant and stable (which human love is not), it would also do what no human love can ever do – it

[1] John 3:16.

would give purpose and meaning to life. It would mean that all the circumstances of your birth, life and death are not caused merely by chance, but that your whole life is in the hands of one who made you in love, and who has a purpose for you which makes sense of all that you are, and which will lead to a complete fulfilment.

Such a love, if it is true, fulfils all the conditions. It comes to you unpursued and unasked. You cannot make God love you, but the Christian gospel says that he does so already. All real love brings with it a sense of unworthiness, and this must be especially true in the case of God's love; yet you discover that God loves you just as you are and for what you are and in spite of anything you may have done. All real love goes on from this point to bring out the very best and highest of which a person is capable. How much more so will this be if God loves you. It can be the beginning of life in a new dimension. A person who is loved finds himself capable of things he never thought possible; a person who is loved finds new qualities which he never possessed before − kindness, unselfishness, generosity, bravery and even heroism. Love makes all things new.

Furthermore, I have written of the need to see life in true perspective. If Christianity is true, then God's love for us, and our response to that love, provide exactly the perspective we need. This is the key which unlocks everything else. When it is put first, then suddenly everything else makes sense and falls into its right place. There is nothing which does not begin to take on real meaning and purpose. There is no question which we have raised so far which cannot be answered. The point is, then, is it true?

4 Faith

We live in days when faith is at a discount. The world is wondering whether it is, in fact, possible to have faith in anything any more. What can you trust nowadays? Whom can you trust? Consult the textbooks or listen to the debates on radio or television and you discover that learned people give entirely different answers to all the important problems of life. This applies equally to science, medicine, economics, politics, religion and all the rest. Who is right?

Our age is one of uncertainty and relativity, and this tends to affect the whole way we think and look at life. In the realm of science, we cannot be absolutely sure, we can deal only in probabilities. In the realm of ethics, we are not even very clear about probabilities. Certainly it is widely doubted whether there are such things as absolute standards. As for politics, expediency is the guiding rule, with the result that election promises have become a standing joke, and international agreements are simply discarded when they prove inconvenient. It used to be said that a man's word was his bond; now, even in a written contract, it is prudent to use a magnifying glass to examine the small print.

We should realize that history has known its great ages of faith. It is just that this is not one of them. It is, rather, an age of scepticism and uncertainty, an age of crisis when everything seems to be in the melting-pot, an age of doubt and of searching for values and for reality. No-one knows quite what is going to happen next. No-one seems to know quite where to put their trust or to lean their weight.

And yet without faith we cannot live. If you had to prove everything before you acted upon it, you would probably never even get out of bed in the morning. If you are sitting on a chair while reading this, you are unconsciously exercising very considerable faith in the strength and property of wood and in the ability of a carpenter or of a machine which you have never even seen. The chair, in its turn, is standing on the floor. But who is to say that the floor will support you? If you get up and walk across the room, the floor-boards may collapse under you. If you are reading this in bed, you will in due course switch off the light and go to sleep without a moment's doubt that tomorrow will really dawn. We are committing ourselves in faith to one thing or another every minute of our lives, sometimes on the evidence of our own experience, sometimes on the basis of other people's experience, and sometimes on the ground of what we believe to be reliable reports. We all have a working faith, whether it has ever been consciously formulated or not. Without it, we would be neurotic and incapable of any action at all.

We should notice here in passing that the strength of our faith is less important than the reliability of the object in which it is placed. I have complete confidence in the chair on which I am now sitting, but if it is badly made, my faith will not prevent me from collapsing on the floor. On the contrary, my faith will add to my peril, because I will be inclined to sit down without due caution!

In days of uncertainty like those in which we are living, people tend to place their faith in things which they can touch and see; it brings a sense of security. The world of ideas and principles seems vague and changing, but in material objects people think they see something immediate and tangible, which gives the impression of stability and permanence. Most people today can face the future with relative equanimity provided they have a steady job, a house, a car, a television and a reasonable bank balance.

Such a faith is perhaps natural, but at the same time very unsatisfactory, because material things are, of all things, the least trustworthy – and we have just seen that it is the reliability of the object, not the strength of the faith, that really matters. Money loses value through inflation; goods quickly become broken and obsolete. The world around us changes rapidly and bewilderingly; no-one knows quite what tomorrow may bring. Certainly if there should be another war on a world scale, then all these material things will suddenly look like useless toys, and if we have put our trust too much in them, the ground will have gone from beneath our feet.

There are certain things which throw a very searching light both on the direction of our faith and on the quality of its object. War, of course, is one: personal loss of someone we love is another; illness is a third;

and, of course, behind them all, like a giant spectre, death is a fourth. It is a frightening experience to realize suddenly in events such as these that all our life we have been placing our faith in something which ultimately will not bear the weight.

But where are we to find the something or someone on which we can place all our faith in the confidence that we shall never be let down? Does such a foundation exist in the midst of a shifting world? Could it be, perhaps, that we are back to the challenge of that haunting verse: 'Set your mind on God's kingdom and his justice before everything else, and all the rest will come to you as well'?[1]

This is, perhaps, a good moment to pause and draw together the main themes of the previous chapters. We began by talking about our purpose in living and of the necessity of finding the keystone which will make sense of everything else. We then proceeded to explore the fact that this keystone must give true value to our lives, making every part contribute to the whole, so that we use every ability and every hour to the full, and develop a complete, integrated and 'valuable' personality. We then saw that the only true measure of our value is to be found in the love of other people for us, and, supremely, in God's unreserved love for us, of which the evidence centres in the life and death of Jesus Christ.

We should now be in a position to see more clearly where faith fits into the picture. To have faith is to rest the whole of one's weight on something or someone in such a way that if it should collapse, we fall with it. To

---

[1] Matthew 6:33, New English Bible.

have faith in a plank is not to admire its solidity from a safe distance, but to step on it. Now if a faith like this is placed squarely in someone who loves us completely (and Christianity tells us that that someone is God), then our lives suddenly take on value, meaning and perspective.

Before we go on to examine more closely the whole question of God and the evidence of his love as shown in the person of Jesus Christ, it is important to understand that faith of the kind I have described in *something* is essential to a full and satisfying life. It is, in fact, the dynamic which gives life direction and power; without it, we inevitably drift. In the modern age, if we have not got a direction of our own, the world will quickly mould us to its own.

No-one has achieved greatness or indeed anything of lasting value without a driving faith in something. Surely the question of where we should place our own faith deserves our most careful consideration. Is it not strange, then, that we spend so little time and thought seeking the right foundation? Everything seems to conspire against it. We tend to pass from one attractive and superficial matter to another as they happen to catch our attention, like a child playing with one brightly coloured toy after another, without stopping to ask what they are really for, or how they fit together. And the danger is that we shall go on doing this until our dying day unless we make the effort to stand back and see things in perspective and find a faith to live by.

Christianity claims to hold the answer to all the key questions we have been asking. But have you ever taken the time and trouble to consider it properly? It claims to make sense of life; it claims to give us an infinite

32

value and an infinite love; it claims to bear the whole weight of our faith and trust; it claims to be the dynamic which will give us the direction and power to live a really worth-while life.

These are staggering claims which need to be investigated. Perhaps you have never done so because you had never really thought about it like this. Perhaps you have never done so because you have a sneaking suspicion that it might be true, and you are not too keen to face that possibility. It is, after all, quite convenient to be a perpetual seeker after truth; it can be used to excuse almost anything.

But let us pursue this question of faith a little further. How are we to assess whether any particular object or person is worthy of the full weight of our trust? Faith is a way of seeing and understanding life. It is not a matter of seeing what is not there; it is a matter of having eyes to see and understand what is there. This means that our faith depends first on the facts that come before our experience, and second on the way we interpret these facts.

We see and experience the world around us every day – people, plants and animals; earth and sky, summer and winter, sun, moon and stars. These are the facts; what is our interpretation? Do we see a giant confusion, or is this God's creation? Do we see a vast series of coincidences, or is there a pattern and a purpose? Turn your gaze back through history and see the vast complex of movements and events. Have they a meaning and a direction, or are they just a tale full of sound and fury, signifying nothing? What of the millions who, all down the ages, have put their trust in God and found him real? Did they grasp reality – or were they deluding themselves? What of the vast numbers of people today who pray to God? Is God really with them, listening to them and answering – or are they just making fools of themselves?

In particular, there are certain specific facts which call for an interpretation on our part. Many, many years ago a man lived what was, by any standards, a remarkable life. He taught some profound truths, which the world has not seemed able to forget. In fact, his life has altered the course of history perhaps more than that of any other man. We are all deeply influenced by him, although probably we are not even aware of it. He died an ignominious death at an early age, but (some said) he rose from death to a new plane of life, because death simply could not hold him. Argument raged around him then, and has continued to rage around him ever since. Some said he was no less than God himself; others said he was either deluded or a fraud.

Now there have been many profound teachers and many good men in the course of history; there have been many unjust executions and many martyrs for the sake of truth. But what makes this man unique are his claims about himself and the incredibly egocentric direction of his teaching. Many have pointed us to God and told us to worship him. Jesus claimed *to be* God and called for faith and commitment to himself. Many have said : There is the truth, follow that. Jesus said : I am the truth – follow me. What is more, his claims carry such conviction that countless numbers in every age and in virtually every nation have taken him at his word. This is, in barest outline, what sets him apart from any other man of stature in history.

What are we to say to this? If what he claimed and

taught is really true, then he holds the answer to your life. That is inescapable, as a little thought will show. If he was just another ordinary man, then he was either an impostor or a sadly deluded person. In that case, to listen to him or follow him can lead to nothing but disillusionment and despair.

Whether Jesus was true or false is not easy to prove in so many words. Certainly it is beyond the scope of this chapter. The point is that faith is a matter of your interpretation of certain facts. Christians would say that the evidence that he is God is strong – overwhelmingly strong. But then different people read the same evidence in different ways. It is up to you to examine it for yourself. What is certain is that Jesus intended you to pin your life and your faith on him as the only one who can give your life purpose and meaning and value. He claimed that that was why he lived and died. If this is true, then he has the answer to your life, and he is the keystone for which you have been seeking. If it is not true, then you must look elsewhere.

You have, then, to examine the evidence and then exercise your faith. You must put your trust either in the fact that Jesus Christ was God and taught the truth, or else you must put your trust in the fact that he was deluded or a fraud. As I said at the beginning, you cannot avoid faith; and, as people have found all down the centuries, you cannot avoid the person of Jesus Christ. He stands astride your path. He said : 'I am the way, and the truth, and the life; no one comes to the Father, but by me.' The Pharisees said : He is misleading the people and deserves to die. What do you say? He deliberately compels us to judge him. Our dating, BC and AD, simply underlines the fact that since he

35

lived and died, no-one can ever be quite the same again.

I am not attempting at this point to state the Christian faith, although I want to make clear how the person of Jesus Christ fits into any discussion on faith. I do want, however, to underline three things. First, that you must have a faith to live by, if your life is to have purpose and meaning and value. Second, that faith results from your interpretation of facts. There are two distinct stages here. You have to decide what is fact and what is not. You cannot base a meaningful life on a vague ideal or feeling. And having sorted out the facts, you then have to interpret them; you have to decide what they mean as far as your life is concerned. Third, having found what you believe to be the true faith, you then have to commit yourself to it, so that it becomes the foundation and driving force in your life.

Many people nowadays say that they have no faith in anything. Even allowing for the fact that this is far from strictly true, it is a counsel of despair. Such people will never make much out of life. Other people *say* they have faith, but it has little effect on their lives. Perhaps they say they believe in God, but it makes no noticeable difference to the way they live. This, of course, is not faith at all, although many people think it is. Faith is not mere assent to certain truths; it is the means to acquire drive, purpose and meaning in life. If it does not fulfil its function, then it is useless.

Where are we to find such a faith? Is it possible to discover a faith adequate for the modern world? Let me briefly summarize the specification. It must be the dynamic which makes life meaningful. It must enable us to enjoy and make the very most of all that is best in life, while being able to discern and reject all that harms and spoils and destroys. It must be a faith that will take us through a world of atomic war, hunger, hatred, disease and fear. It must be a faith which will one day (and it might, of course, be any day) take us through death itself to whatever lies beyond. We have only one life. Nothing less will do.

5 God

There are two problems which must be considered here. The first concerns the existence and the character of God; the second is whether such a God can be the key to a faith to live by. In other words, if Christianity is right in what it affirms about God, does this help towards providing the basis for a meaningful life in terms of the specification in the last chapter?

The New Testament never questions the existence of God – it assumes it as a fundamental fact of life. Jesus Christ never questioned the existence of God; indeed (and this is a matter which will require your most careful consideration) he claimed to be in such a close, constant and unique relationship with God that he could say, 'I and the Father are one'.[1] Furthermore, he claimed to be the means God has used to reveal himself to mankind. He said, in effect, that he had come to show us what God is like; that as we look at him, we see God, and as we believe in him, we believe in God.

[1] John 10:30.

Indeed, if we do not believe in God when we look at Jesus and what he did, then it is unlikely that we will ever believe in God at all.

What Jesus is saying here is breathtaking in its sheer audacity. No wonder we are forced to make up our minds about him. He is doing what no ordinary man in his right senses (and certainly no ordinary good man) could possibly dare to do. He is making *himself* the test of the existence and the character of God. He is taking all the arguments for and against God, and calmly lifting them on to an entirely different and personal plane. 'Who do you say that I am?' he inquires,[1] inviting us to examine him in the closest detail, to see if we can discover any flaw in his character, if we can question his authority, or explain away his power and his deeds, whether we can challenge the fact or the meaning of his death and resurrection. And at the end of it all, he asks simply: Do you believe in me? Do you trust me? I am telling you the truth when I say that God is your Father who loves you, and that you can come to him by way of me and find new life. I am the truth.

The character of Christ's claim seems more than a little devastating at first sight. It all seems a little too simple and a little too bold. But if God had wanted us to know that he exists, and at the same time to make it a matter to which we must make a personal commitment of faith, could he have found a more effective way?

I am not going to try to prove to you that there is a God. Proof is a very elusive thing. I would be hard put

[1] Mark 8:29.

to prove even that I exist, and I am told of the philosophy lecturer who asked his students to prove that they were not dreaming. Discussions which set out to prove that God either does or does not exist invariably run aground here, or to be more exact, they get lost in thin air. Christ's claim is so compelling precisely because he brings the whole matter down to earth, and suddenly it becomes a matter of personal response and faith. Only the most intellectual can engage in subtle philosophical debate, and even then it tends to lead nowhere in the end. But Jesus Christ is someone whom anyone can understand and to whom anyone can respond. The existence of God becomes a matter not of intellect alone, but also of heart and will.

Nevertheless there are three useful lines of approach which we can explore at this stage before we come back to the person and the claims of Jesus Christ. I want, first, to suggest the *probability* that there is a God; second, to look at what we might reasonably expect of a God who loves us; and then, third, to see whether what we might reasonably expect is, in fact, borne out in people's practical experience.

First, then, let us look at the probability that there is a God. This probability is derived partly from our observation and experience of the universe we live in, and partly from our experience of ourselves and the human personality. We look at the universe and find it hard to believe that there is no first cause or creator. It may seem philosophically naïve, but it is nevertheless natural to ask simply, where did it all come from? Again, as we look at the world, we feel that it requires not only a creator, but an explanation. We ask what it all means, and we find that the answer does not seem to be contained within the universe itself, but lies beyond it. Furthermore, we see order, consistency, and apparently rational design. Can this be the outcome of mere accident and chance? Does it not imply a creative mind? And what is the purpose of it all? Can it be that the answer is really nothing at all?

If we turn from our observation of the world to our experience of ourselves and the human personality, here also we find distinct features which appear to argue for the existence of a God. We find within ourselves a moral consciousness expressed in the word 'ought', which, in spite of many attempts, seems to defy analysis except in terms of a higher moral being. We find that man is capable of the very deepest religious and spiritual experience, a knowledge of something far beyond himself; an encounter or glimpse of ultimate reality, at which moments he seems to be most truly himself, and that he has an idea or concept in his mind of perfection which could hardly be there at all unless it corresponds to some reality.

The various classical arguments for the existence of God arise out of these various observations and experiences of man. As arguments they are, of course, susceptible to philosophical debate *ad infinitum* and, indeed, *ad nauseam*. It is important not to claim too much for them (they are *arguments*, not proofs), but their combined weight is very impressive, and they have a way of emerging from even the most damaging attack just as fresh and curiously convincing as ever. Taken together, they certainly suggest the strong probability that there is a God and that he is good. Beyond that we cannot go. It would seem that God has given us in his creation certain pointers, but no conclusive proofs; we are encouraged to believe in him, but not forced to do so. This is consistent with the Christian's view of his purpose for men, as we shall see in a moment.

I have mentioned here the classical arguments for the existence of God, without pausing to state them in any detail. This is not a textbook in any sense of the word, and those who are seriously concerned with the problem of the existence of God will easily find such a statement elsewhere, and they should study it with great care.[1] In this book I am trying to avoid details, and to keep to general lines of thought. I am concerned with pointers, rather than with specific points. I am more anxious to raise questions than to answer them. The Christian answers can be obtained in any good Christian book on the subject (and there is a suggested reading list on page 96); it is being interested enough to ask the questions that matters in the first place. It is tragic if Christianity is dismissed by anyone without careful thought and investigation. Too often this happens merely because of prejudice, neglect, or sometimes an unfortunate childhood experience. If I can persuade anyone that the claims and teaching of Jesus Christ are worth unbiased and careful study on their own merits, then this book will have fulfilled its purpose.

We have looked, then, at the probability that there is a God. Let us now turn to ask what we might reasonably expect of such a God. We should notice, first of

[1] For a clear, short statement of the arguments in their context, see, for example, Chapter I of *Christian Doctrine* by J. S. Whale (Fontana).

all, that we should *not* expect to understand all about him with our own unaided reason. People will sometimes reject the idea of God because they cannot pin him down, and make him behave in accordance with their own ideas and preconceptions. An argument will quite often begin with a phrase to the effect that, *if* there were a God, he would (or would not) do something. But if God is indeed the creator of the universe and of ourselves, then that puts him straight away far beyond the range of our minds. If we could understand him, or legislate for him, or reduce him to a logical proposition, then he would not be God at all.

But if it is inevitable from the nature of things that we cannot possibly reach God, then how are we to know him? Clearly the answer is that if he wants us to know him at all, then he must reveal himself to us. If we cannot cross the gap to him, then he must cross the gap to us. This is what we should expect, and this is, in fact, what we find in Christianity. This is what makes it so different from other religions. It is not man who is seeking God (because it is impossible that he should ever find him in any full sense), but God who is seeking man.

Furthermore, if we are to grasp what it is God wants us to know, then we should expect him to state it in human terms, just as a teacher must express himself in terms which a child can understand, if truth is to be communicated. Again, this is what we find in Christianity. 'The Word became flesh and dwelt among us.'[1] God's message to man was expressed in terms of a human life; in terms of a baby born at Bethlehem, of a

---

[1] John 1:14.

man who lived a perfect human life and taught in parables so that the ordinary people heard and understood him gladly; in terms of love and healing and forgiveness for men and women; of bread and wine shared among those who loved him; in terms of a death on a cross one Friday morning, which he said was for us – and of a resurrection on a Sunday, which he said was for us as well.

If God really wanted us to understand that he loves us and wants us to share our life with him, could he possibly have chosen a more simple, eloquent and direct way? Why, even a child can understand it, if he is not too proud.

Perhaps this strikes you as being altogether beneath the dignity of a God who is the creator of all things. But the keystone of Christ's life and teaching is that God *loves* us, and the one thing which real love can never do is to stand upon dignity. Supposing that you love someone who cares nothing for you and ignores your existence. You may decide that the only thing to do is to go and tell that person about your love, hoping and longing for a response. It is no good being proud. You run the risk of being laughed at and spurned. You are laying yourself open to being terribly hurt. But it is the only way – and God chose that way at Calvary, when Christ was crucified.

What more would we expect? If God wants us to respond to his love and give ourselves to him, then clearly he wants a free and not a forced response. I said earlier that the lack of final proof for the existence of God is consistent with the Christian viewpoint. If God could be conclusively proved, then we would have no option but to believe in him. But such a forced acknowledgment, with its inevitable demand for worship and obedience, stifles the free response of love. We can be made to obey, but we cannot be made to love against our will. If God really wants us as his children and not as his puppets or slaves, then he is bound to leave it finally to us whether we will have him or not. This is what we must expect, and, again, this is what we do, in fact, find. God lays his love open before us through the life and death of Jesus Christ, and promises us every good thing if we will have him. But he will not force his way in unasked. We can turn him away if we insist.

God's problem, if I can put it in this way, was to reveal himself to mankind in such a way that we can respond to him in love and commitment, without at the same time so completely overwhelming us that a free response becomes impossible. He had to give sufficient evidence of his existence and his love so that anyone with eyes to see and a heart to understand would look, and believe, and respond. But there had to be room for man to exercise his will; there had to be the genuine possibility of turning away from him. God's answer to this problem of self-revelation was, the Christian believes, the person of Jesus Christ.

What, then, would we expect man's response to be? If God, by the very nature of his approach, does not force us to turn to him, would we nevertheless expect every man to come willingly and eagerly? If you are tempted to answer immediately Yes, then pause a moment and look at yourself. Love can be very demanding; it implies time, service, loyalty and unselfishness. It means living for another, rather than for yourself. At the moment, you run your own life in your own way. Would you be willing to transfer your loyalty to God, if he exists – to make him the centre of your life, instead of yourself? Would you be willing, in fact, for God to start taking control of your life and giving you that faith to live by which we looked at earlier?

I do not know how you are answering these questions. Perhaps you are longing for that kind of faith and life. What I do know is that many, many people are so obsessed with their own selves and with their own desire for independence that they lose all capacity for real love, which finds its true meaning in self-forgetfulness and in self-giving.

Pride is another deadly enemy of love. People are too proud to accept God's offer of love and help and power, or they are determined to struggle through life by themselves, even if it does mean ultimate defeat. Often people will humble themselves sufficiently to turn to God when they are in trouble or sorrow, but will resolutely refuse to have anything to do with him when things are going well. Apathy is yet another enemy. Many people do not really want to face the demands of love or of a living faith at all. They prefer to drift and to try to enjoy the moments as they come, even if it does mean that they never find real happiness or satisfaction. No – I do not think we should expect to find everyone responding to a God of love. Love is too demanding and inconvenient; it requires self-giving, humility and effort.

We have looked, then, at what we might expect to find if God exists and if Christ's teaching about his character is true. I think it is not too much to claim that Christianity shows itself here to be consistent and reasonable. We now turn to what might be called the acid test. Does this theory work out in practice? Does Christianity work? If there really is no God, then surely a person would very soon discover it and be disillusioned: his faith simply would not work.

The sheer weight, variety and range of Christian testimony is extremely impressive – of that there is no doubt. People of every age and type and temperament, from virtually every tribe and nation in the world, over a period of two thousand years, have borne witness by their life, by their lips, by their writings, and not infrequently by their death, that there is a God, and that he does love us, and that faith in him truly is the dynamic which makes sense and reality of life. Such testimony is not easily ignored or explained away. Nor yet is it merely subjective. Evidence for the existence and love of God is written on the lives of men and women. You do not need to search very far to find people who have been turned from despair and failure to joy and purpose; from crime and debauchery, from which there seemed no escape, to new life and freedom; from hatred to love; people who have found strength to live through incredible hardship and suffering, and who have proved God for themselves, even if they could not state it scientifically. This is the sort of practical evidence which you should examine for yourself. You can read it for yourself in books of Christian biography, or go and find a Christian and ask him about his own experience and his evidence that God is real.

We have looked, in very broad outline, at some of the evidence for the reality and the character of God. There is the probability of his existence derived from our observation and experience of the world and of ourselves. There is the consistency of the Christian gospel with what we might reasonably expect from God, if he does exist. Third, there is the tremendous range and depth of human evidence in people's lives and experience. And this all finds its focal point, for the Christian, in the life and personality of one man, Jesus Christ, who invites us still, if we doubt the reality of God, to look at him and judge for ourselves.

We must now go on to examine the second question I posed earlier. If God really exists, and his character is truly what Christ taught us that it is, then does this really provide the key to our lives? Does it, in fact, do anything to fulfil the conditions laid down at the end of the last chapter for a faith by which to live? If we acknowledge that God is real, what difference will this make to our lives?

I said earlier that the keystone of Christ's life and teaching is that God loves us – loves each one of us with a love that will not let us go. God, he told us, does not love just good people, he loves all people. God does not just love mankind in general, he loves *you* in particular.

Now it is possible that we have heard this so often that it does not seem to mean very much. If this is so, then sit back for a moment and try to take it in. Of all personal relationships, love is the one which most demands a response of one kind or another. No-one can simply say, 'I see', and carry on as before. Merely to take note of it as a bare fact or statement is to show that one simply has not understood at all. Now if this is true on the human level, how much more is it true where God is concerned. Christ proclaimed that God, the creator of the universe, the supreme being in whom all things centre, *loves you*. This must be the most amazing statement ever made. If it is true, then your life can never be quite the same again. We have already taken note of the fact that what we need most of all is to be loved – not for what we have, nor for what we pretend to be, but simply for what we are. If we are really loved by God, then this must inevitably revolutionize our lives.

Love gives value, as we have seen. How incredible, then, if God himself, who knows all about us, including our innermost thoughts and desires, really thinks us of such immense value. This is far more than to say that he is interested in us. Many people believe that and find it either frightening or of no consequence. Christ said that God loves us, and that can only mean that we are worth more in God's eyes than we could ever have imagined.

Some people value themselves too high, and others too low; both sorts of people sell themselves too cheaply, as we have seen. Other people's valuation of us may give a truer and more sober estimate, and when we do discover that someone else loves us, we can hardly believe that it is true. But the most important valuation of all is God's valuation. What does he think of us? The Christian answer is that God showed his love for us in unmistakable terms, by his willingness to pay the very highest possible price for us on the cross. 'Herein is love, not that we loved God, but that he loved us, and sent his Son to be the propitiation for our sins.'[1] Christ's death on the cross for you is the highest price, and consequently the highest valuation, that has ever been put on your life.

God's love for us gives us not only value, but mean-

---

[1] 1 John 4 : 10, Authorized Version.

ing and purpose. We see something of this in human relationships. If we become aware that someone really loves us and we respond with our own love and self-giving, then suddenly we have something to live for. Suddenly it matters how we get on and how we behave. Suddenly we see beauty and our lives fill with joy. Love is the difference between real life and mere existence.

Now if this is true on the human level, how much more it proves to be true when God loves us. Human love may disappoint us, or may evade us altogether. Human love is capable of bringing even more misery than happiness. Human love is, by its very nature, transitory. At its best and highest, it is a most wonderful thing, but it can never answer the deepest needs and longings of the heart. It can never be a faith to live by.

The last chapter laid down stringent requirements for such a faith. If it is really true that God loves us personally and has a purpose for us, then this would answer every one of those requirements. It would give meaning and value and the essential driving power. It would mean that our life is moving from a real beginning to a real end. It would mean that we are in the hands of someone who can give us all the things in life which are for our highest good and keep us from everything that will spoil and destroy; someone who knows our deepest needs and desires, because he made us, and who has power to meet them all. It would mean that we are in the hands of someone who can take us through atomic war, through hunger or disease, yes, even through death itself.

If Christianity is true, then it has the answer to life. The way to discover whether it is true or not is first by investigating the Christian gospel with care and humility, and then, second, actually by putting God to the test in your own life – not arrogantly, of course, but humbly committing yourself to him if he exists and asking him to take your life and make something of it, and to show you, so far as you are able to understand it and take it in, the fullness and the reality of his existence and love for you.

God's love demands the response of our whole personality. His approach to us requires a decision. He promises that as we respond and follow and obey, we will discover for ourselves who he is and what he can do for us.

6 Sin

This title may sound a little forbidding. Christians are sometimes thought to be obsessed with the subject of sin (which some people seem to equate with sex!), and it may be that you have been waiting for me to tell you that we are all sinners. Being a Christian is even thought to mean wearing a long face and a dark suit and studiously avoiding anything you enjoy – rather like believing medicine can be good for you only if it tastes nasty! If Christians ever give this impression they are, needless to say, missing the whole point of their faith. Jesus Christ promises us a life which is in every sense *better* (not worse) than the one we have already, and unless this is true, Christianity has clearly nothing to offer the world. Fortunately the idea that Christianity is morbid or repressive does not emanate from Jesus Christ at all, nor from the Bible, and we do well to examine the subject for ourselves.

In fact, I do not want to begin by talking about *behaviour* at all, but about our relationship with God. We saw in the last chapter that, in the Christian view, the life and death of Jesus Christ were God's means of showing us his reality and his love for us. But we cannot leave the matter there, because this is only half the story. Christ claimed that his death was not only the means of showing us God's love, but also of putting right a relationship which had gone wrong.

Exactly what it is that has gone wrong in our relationship with God can be seen very clearly in four concepts raised in the last chapter: God's existence, and his character, man's free will, and his desire for independence. Needless to say, God's existence is the prerequisite of any kind of relationship with him at all, but if you accept the fact that he exists, then it becomes relevant to ask what your attitude to him has been all your life. Probably you have ignored him altogether, perhaps even scoffed at him. Perhaps you have paid him some formal acknowledgment, but can that be in any way adequate for *God*? The defence is, of course, that this was done out of ignorance. But will this really stand examination? In this country there is a Bible in virtually every household and a church on almost every corner. It is hardly possible that anyone who really wants to know about God does not know about him. The trouble is, of course, that most people simply do not want to know. God is wilfully ignored.

The matter becomes even more serious when we go on to consider God's character. It is not merely God's existence that is ignored, but his love. We know from human experience that there is nothing which hurts more than to have one's love ignored or rejected. What it means to God to be hurt in this way it is hard for us to imagine, although clearly his capacity to be hurt cannot be *less* than human. But we do get a glimpse of what our rejection means to God when we consider Christ's death on the cross. We can begin to see there just what man does to perfect, self-giving love which is the ground of all reality. Between God and man there is a relationship which is wrong indeed.

This relationship has not gone wrong from God's side – that much is clear. So we come to consider man's free will and his desire for independence. We have seen already that man's free response to God is essential to God's plan. This means that our rejection of God's love must be a genuine possibility – and that we have been taking advantage of that possibility for years. We have been keeping God out of our lives because we are frightened of losing our independence. In so doing, we have been ignoring his existence and rejecting his love. This is the basis of what the Christian means by the word 'sin'.

Man has used his free will to become totally self-centred, to make himself the centre of his own world, and this has become a natural part of the human make-up. This is what makes it so deadly and so hard to combat. We can see something of just how natural it is when we look at a baby or a young child. Many people apparently think that a baby cannot be 'sinful' because he has no knowledge of right or wrong. But observe a baby who is in any way frustrated or who fails to obtain something he wants. His tiny fists clench, his face becomes red, and eventually purple, his eyes screw up, his legs kick, and when he has sufficient breath, he lets out a bellow of rage which rises in pitch until his desires are satisfied !

Granted that this is partly a form of self-protection, it would nevertheless be hard to paint a more accurate picture of human nature. We have a built-in obsession with ourselves; we know what we want and we will get it if we can; our interest in the world is mostly confined to what we can get out of it, and we become extremely frustrated if we cannot make circumstances serve our own ends. When faced with God's authority and the challenge of his love, therefore, our natural reaction is to say No at any cost. We are self-centred, when we ought to be God-centred, and we have no desire to change. The idea of living for something or someone other than ourselves, and hence letting control of our lives pass out of our own hands, is frankly terrifying. Indeed, if we face up to it squarely and understand what it means, it seems like a kind of death.

Is it possible that man can change? Supposing that we recognize the existence and the claims of God and long for a right relationship with him with all that it must bring, can we begin a new life with a new centre and a new focus? This is man's problem. The Christian gospel is that Jesus Christ came to provide the answer.

This is not the place for a full exposition of the gospel, for which I hope you will be concerned enough to seek elsewhere,[1] but if the situation I have described is correct then there are two basic things we need if we are to live a full, positive life in a right relationship with God : the first is God's forgiveness for the past, when we have wilfully kept him out of our lives; and the second is a new power which will enable us to live life in the way he wants in the future. The Christian claim is that the death of Jesus Christ on the cross has shown for all time God's willingness to forgive us, and more

[1] See, *e.g.*, *Basic Christianity* by John R. W. Stott (IVF).

than that, has actually secured forgiveness for all who seek it; and that his resurrection from the dead and the promised gift of his Spirit to all who put their trust in him guarantees us the power we need for the future.

We should now be in a position to see something of how the word 'sin' applies to personal behaviour and to the whole field of Christian ethics and social problems. To take the question of personal behaviour first, this is a subject we find very hard to face squarely. We have a distinct dislike for set rules of conduct and we virtually like to claim the right to make up our own rules as we go along. We rebel instinctively against any authority which tries to enforce rules, especially when they are not (to our mind) adequately explained. And in any case we tend to regard our behaviour as our own personal matter in which no-one has the right to interfere. There must be few who do not feel this way, at least to some extent; it is the mood and the outlook of our time.

This makes us suspicious of Christianity, even if we do believe in God, because we fear that our lives may be run for us, and restricted within a rigid set of rules. But we ought now to be able to look at this in a new light. I have tried to indicate that we are self-centred when we ought to be God-centred. This is the root-cause of what goes wrong with all our personal relationships, and it is, incidentally, the point of that very illuminating story of the garden of Eden. Man no longer obeys God; he follows his own inclination, believing that he can become fully independent. If this is so, then no wonder we want to make up our own rules of conduct. Our main object in life is to achieve what we believe to be best for ourselves.

But supposing that we become Christians by committing ourselves in faith to Jesus Christ. His promise is that we can then begin a new life with God at the centre. This means a complete change in outlook and attitude. It is not a matter of simply obeying a set of rigid rules; it is a matter of responding in obedience to a God who loves us. This may look on the surface as if it means that we can never make the most of life for ourselves. On the contrary, says Christ, this is the only way to get the very best out of life. Your own way is self-defeating in the end; God's way guarantees you complete fulfilment, first, because he knows exactly your potentialities and your deepest desires (after all, he *made* you), and second, because he has the power to use and satisfy them to the full.

The basis of personal behaviour, then, lies in obedient response to God's will, simply because we believe that he loves us and knows what he is doing. Of course, to know what his will is in any given situation is not always easy, but he does promise to guide us definitely and personally. How he does so in actual practice is beyond the scope of this chapter, although prayer and the right use of the Bible spring to mind as two of the most obvious ways, but the best line of approach that can be given here is simply to say : If you want to know whether God will guide you, ask him to do so, give him the opportunity and be willing to do what he tells you, and then see for yourself.

Let us now look briefly at how the word 'sin' applies to the wider field of Christian ethics and social problems. Our 'world consciousness' today has given us, in the West at least, something of a 'world conscience'.

People are concerned, as perhaps never before, with the vast social and economic problems which exist in many parts of the world. Many people who do not profess to be Christians in any sense find themselves moved to give of their time and their money, sometimes even to give their careers, to help alleviate these problems. Possibly they never go inside a church, but they are prepared to go to almost any lengths to help the hungry, the poor and the homeless of the world. To them it may seem grossly unfair to be called totally self-centred, even if they make no claim to be God-centred; they succeed, at any rate some of the time, in looking away from themselves to their fellow men.

Part of the misunderstanding which arises here comes from regarding huge social problems, such as that which exists in India, for example, as in some way basically different from the individual human problem we looked at earlier in the chapter. In fact, the difference is mainly one of size, not of type. This is the problem of personal sin writ large.

If we believe in a God of love, then it does not take much to see that the world is very far from what he must want it to be. This is not a reflection on his power, but on the use man has made of his free will, which, as we have seen, it was inevitable that God should give us. Men have taken this free will and, instead of using it to live as the children of God, have sought to turn it to their own advantage. Inevitably the world becomes a battlefield of competition, with everyone trying to obtain the best of limited resources for themselves. Moreover, there is competition on the human as well as the material level, as everyone seeks to use his neighbour to serve his own ends. The world has remarkably few

58

purely natural problems; mostly they are human ones – the result of greed and selfishness. There is probably enough food in the world for everyone, if it were equally shared out. What deficiency there is could be made good, perhaps for all time, if scientists and others really co-operated on an international scale to serve the needs of others. Probably the same could be said of housing and medicine, and of other fields as well. Much is being done already by a minority, but the problem is not primarily one of politics, nor of organization, nor of education, but of the human heart.

War breaks out in one part of the world after another; one problem is solved only to be replaced by a different and equally difficult one. People tend to think that surely the answer lies in either more armament or more disarmament; in a better government, or at least in a different government; in a tougher line of negotiation, or in a complete withdrawal. But the truth is that so long as men are interested only in themselves – their own comfort, wealth and convenience, and their own ends – then there is bound to be war, and any temporary solution will treat the symptoms and not the disease.

I said just now that if we believe in a God of love, then it does not take much to see that the world is very far from what he must want it to be. We can go further than that. It must be that such a God has a complete and wonderful purpose for this world. If his will for this world were being implemented by man, then there would be no war, no hunger, no refugees; there would be no greed, no hatred and no selfishness. Indeed the Christian belief in a God of love tells us clearly that such a day is really coming. But if man is to play his part in this, then we are back inevitably to the question of our own response to the call of God in Jesus Christ. Only if we are willing to forsake our own way (the way of 'sin'), and commit ourselves to doing God's will, can we possibly make a constructive contribution to God's plan for this world.

How do we do it? First, we must put ourselves in a right relationship with God, by claiming the forgiveness which Jesus Christ won for us on the cross, when selfishness and greed were exposed in their true light, and love won for ever the victory over human sin. Second, we must place ourselves unreservedly in God's hands, so that we may play our part in fulfilling his perfect will for the world, by following the example and by claiming the power of Jesus Christ. Third, we must follow Christ as his disciples to win others for the cause of God, that the time may truly come when 'sin', either in its personal or world-wide manifestations, is banished from the earth.

There should by now be emerging from all our discussion a clear idea of the absolute centrality of Jesus Christ to the Christian faith. It is essential to understand this clearly if we are ever to grasp what Christianity means. Many people think they know what it is all about when in reality they have little or no idea. This is often because they are looking at the church, at the clergy, or even at history, when they should be looking at Jesus Christ. He is our main evidence for the existence and the love of God. He is the one who, by his life and death, made possible our forgiveness, and now offers us a new beginning and a new basis for living in obedience and response to the will of God. He is the one who promises to be our leader, guide and helper, if we will place our faith entirely in him, and who will give us the ability to live the full and satisfying life for which God created us. He is the one who said he would come to judge the earth, and bring to pass that day when 'sin', with all that it entails, shall be no more. By him Christianity stands or falls.

Being a Christian, then, is not a matter merely of obeying certain moral precepts, or of living a certain kind of life, or of going to church. It is a matter of personal response and commitment to one who comes to each of us, as he did to the disciples by the lakeside, and calls: 'Come, follow me.' And as we hear his call, we must decide either to remain mending our nets and going about our daily lives without him, seeking only our own ends; or we must rise and follow, not knowing where he will lead us, but believing that only in him can we find a faith to live by.

The call of Jesus Christ demands choice and commitment. But before we look at this more closely, there are one or two other aspects of the Christian life which we must examine.

7 Peace

The Christian is often heard to talk about the peace which his faith brings, but there is a fruitful source of misunderstanding here. A common reaction is for a person to retort: 'I don't want peace in my life, I want adventure and excitement. Peace sounds much too dull.'

This difficulty mainly arises from the fact that the word 'peace' has become a jargon word which can have a whole variety of meanings. For example, it is frequently used today in the purely negative sense of 'absence of war' and this shows the word watered down almost to nothing.[1] In the particular reaction quoted above, the assumption is that the word 'peace' implies the opposite of adventure and excitement. But is this really so? Surely peace implies the opposite of fear, worry and instability. No-one, so far as I know, wants their life to be full of these.

Let us try to give some positive content to the word

[1] See chapter 9 of William Barclay's *The Plain Man looks at the Beatitudes* (Fontana).

'peace'. In the Christian sense, a person who has peace in himself has an inner stability, harmony and joy which nothing can disturb. Now there is not a person in the world today who does not need these. This is the quality from which springs confidence, health and happiness. There is probably no disease or mental illness which is not caused or aggravated by lack of it. In the last chapter we considered the problem of war, but cannot the lack of peace on earth so often be traced back ultimately to lack of peace in the hearts of men and women?

If, once more, we base our thinking on the existence and the character of God, then a certain order of priorities becomes apparent. First of all, it is necessary for us to attain peace with God; this will result in peace in our own hearts and lives; and this, in turn, will issue in peaceful relationships with other people. Let us look at these three stages in turn.

If you look carefully and honestly at your relationship with God, I wonder what you find. It may be anything from open hostility, through cold war to positive peace. One thing is certain, as we saw in the previous chapter; we are not naturally at peace with God. There is not one of us who does not want to run our own life without his intervention if we possibly can, and until we decide to surrender our lives to him, there is bound to be an uneasy relationship which is far from peaceful. Of how this can be put right I have already given some indication. Suffice it to say here that, since Christ died on the cross, there is nothing which stands in the way of our peace with God except our own pride and rebellious nature. If we really want peace, even this can be overcome.

What is more, not only can this relationship of peace be established, it can also be maintained. Too often being a Christian is thought of as a rather risky business depending entirely on the goodness of our own life. On this view our standing with God breaks down every time we do wrong, with the result that we are constantly falling in and out of favour with God. If this were so, we could never know any real peace from one minute to the next. Fortunately the New Testament teaches us something quite different. It tells us that God remains faithful even when we are disloyal, and that to become a Christian is to enter into a permanent relationship with God which nothing can shake. Christians believe that Jesus Christ won a complete victory for us on the cross, and although we sometimes lose our peace of mind because of our own failures, our standing with God is for ever secure, and in this we can have complete and permanent confidence.

To establish peace with God is, the Christian believes, the one sure way to achieve a basis for peace in our hearts and lives. If we lack peace because there are things in our past which have gone wrong and which cannot now be put right, we can be assured of complete forgiveness, and given the chance of a new beginning. If we lack peace because we are lonely and unsure of ourselves, then we can know what it means to be accepted and to be valued by God just for what we are. If we lack peace because we are worried about the future, we can be sure that we will have the guidance and the power of God, and that not even death can separate us from his love. These are the things which give a person true peace, balance and confidence within himself.

This, in its turn, provides the basis for right relationships with other people, because a right relationship is a peaceful one. Note again, however, that peace is positive and not merely negative. It is not at all a case of merely agreeing with everybody and avoiding disputes. Peace is a source of strength, not of weakness. The inner stability of which we have been speaking enables the Christian to approach his neighbour from a position of confidence and strength, and his inner peace finds its expression in outgoing love, which is (and has been demonstrated to be) the most powerful force in the world.

Many people seek to bring peace to the world today and by a whole variety of methods. But in the last resort it is only those who *have* peace within themselves who are capable of *bringing* peace to anyone else. The trouble with most efforts for peace in the world is that they spring from fear, not from love, and that they desire not positive peace but negative absence of war. This applies both to those who rely on atomic weapons and to those who demonstrate against them. But the person who has peace can give peace. The person who has stability and harmony within himself takes them with him wherever he goes. He brings these qualities into every situation and every encounter just by being himself. This is the power of God at work in the world to bring about reconciliation and a new relationship of love and understanding between those of different temperament, class, colour, or ideology. This is no quick or easy answer to the world's problems. But no solution is either valid or permanent which does not both begin and end in the heart and mind of man. It is here that an entirely new attitude must come about if any proposed course of action is to have a chance of success, and the only one who can achieve such a change is God himself. With his help, a person can succeed in bringing a true peace into the world beyond his wildest dreams.

I want to end this chapter by looking at four common misconceptions about the character of a man who has peace within himself. First, he need never be *dull*. Many people seem to think that peace involves inaction, but this is not so. A machine which is working correctly within itself, and which is properly adjusted to the machinery around it, can be said to be at peace, no matter how fast it happens to be working. The right engagement of parts leads, not to lifelessness, but to speed, efficiency and the minimum of wear. A man can be very busy and may efficiently get through an enormous amount of work, but he can still be at peace. It is the secret of success and health.

The following variation on the theme of the twenty-third psalm by a Japanese student, Toki Miyashina, makes the point :

The Lord is my Pace-setter, I shall not rush.
He makes me stop and rest for quiet intervals,
He provides me with images of stillness, which restore my serenity.
He leads me in ways of efficiency, through calmness of mind,
And His guidance is peace.
Even though I have a great many things to accomplish each day
I will not fret, for His presence is here,
His timelessness, His all-importance will keep me in balance.
He prepares refreshment and renewal in the midst of my activity
By anointing my mind with His oils of tranquillity;

My cup of joyous energy overflows.
Surely harmony and effectiveness shall be the fruits of my
hours,
For I shall walk in the pace of my Lord, and dwell in His
house for ever.

Second, the man of peace need not be a *reactor*.
Most people depend for their mood and happiness on
the people and the atmosphere around them. They
react to certain people and situations in a certain given
way. But there are just a few people who do not react
to atmosphere – they create it.

I heard once of a man who bought a newspaper outside a station, and although his smile and friendly
'Good evening' were returned with a scowl and a curse,
he walked away happy and composed. A friend who
was with him remarked, 'If he had done that to me I
would have lost my temper' – an immediate reaction
difficult to avoid. But the man replied, 'Why should I
let him determine the way I am going to behave?' We
need to develop a personality which is integrated and
consistent, and which depends as little as possible on
outside circumstances. The man of peace has the
balance and stability to be himself, whatever may
happen.

Third, he need never be *frightened*. There is much
fear in the world today, and it is fear which is respon-
sible for so much of the world's evil and unhappiness.
It comes in many ways: fear of war; fear of other
people; fear of oneself – of weakness, or failure; fear of
being laughed at, of loneliness and of death. Fear is
what prevents most people ever being truly themselves.
Fear is what prevents so many people ever living as
they really long to live.

But the Christian can have peace within himself because he knows that he is never alone, and that, with God, there can be no such thing as real failure. As for being weak, this is paradoxically his greatest strength. If we have strength of our own we will use it and rely on it, and one day someone will come along who is stronger than we are, or a situation will arise which is beyond us, and then we will know both fear and failure. But if we know that no strength of our own will be adequate in the end, and we are willing to experience the strength and presence of God, then we can know true peace, even in the face of war or death.

As St Paul realized long ago : 'If God is for us, who is against us? ... Who shall separate us from the love of Christ? Shall tribulation, or distress, or persecution, or famine, or nakedness, or peril, or sword? ... No, in all these things we are more than conquerors through him who loved us. For I am sure that neither death, nor life, nor angels, nor principalities, nor things present, nor things to come, nor powers, nor height, nor depth, nor anything else in all creation, will be able to separate us from the love of God in Christ Jesus our Lord.'[1]

Lastly, the man who has peace in himself will not be *hurt*. We speak of a person being hurt in three ways. His body can be hurt by material objects and by disease. Feelings can be hurt by other people's attitudes and lack of love. The soul can be hurt by being cut off from God who is the source of its life.

God can, and sometimes does, prevent us from being hurt bodily. Probably we have no idea of the extent to which he does. But this is not the kind of harm which

---

[1] Romans 8:31, 35, 37-39.

ultimately matters. To have one's feelings hurt can be much more painful. If we lay our love open to others we are probably bound to get hurt and sometimes badly hurt. This is the pain which Jesus Christ experienced more acutely than anyone else has ever done, because his love was perfect. If we really have peace within ourselves, this kind of hurt can never be fatal, although we all experience it. It is the hurt to the soul which is really fatal, and it is in this sense that I say that the Christian need never experience it. Peace with God means that no hurt need ever be truly fatal.

Missionaries sometimes come home and have to tell of how they were beaten, tortured or starved. They go out of love for people and sometimes they are killed for their trouble. Yet their testimony is incredible. Nearly always they report that they were not *hurt* – not, that is, in any way which ultimately matters, and we have already noted the supreme importance of being able to tell the difference between what really matters and what, in the end, does not matter at all.

Jesus said : 'Peace I leave with you; my peace I give to you; not as the world gives do I give to you. Let not your hearts be troubled, neither let them be afraid.'[1] This is the peace which the world can neither give nor ever take away, no matter what may happen to you. It is the peace which comes through a right relationship with God.

[1] John 14:27.

8 Freedom

Lying deep-rooted in our human nature – and it has been lying just beneath the surface of much of our discussion so far – is a basic objection to Christianity which you might state like this: 'I don't want to live under God's control. I want to run my own life in freedom and independence. Even if I do make a mess of it, at least it will be my own effort.' You say, in other words, that you are free and that you are frightened of becoming a slave. Jesus Christ replies: On the contrary, you are a slave. I have come to make you free.

Let us look, first of all, in a little detail at your own claim to be free. If by freedom you mean the ability to do exactly what you like, then probably nobody has ever been free. I began this book by pointing out that your heredity and environment have already determined much of your capability and temperament. This narrows the scope of your so-called freedom very considerably. You simply never will do many of the things you dream about because of the accidents of geography, temperament and ability.

When you really get down to detail, there are, for example, probably only a very few careers open to you; you must choose one. There is not too much freedom here, and, in any case, who says you will choose right? There are probably only one or two girls you are ever likely to meet who would consider marrying you (or *vice versa* if you are a girl). You may never meet any of them. Your real freedom is very limited indeed, and again who is to say that you will use the freedom you have to make the right choice?

Again, if you try to do exactly what you want, you very soon find other barriers inconveniently in the way. The law, money and other people are just three of them. The range of your possible freedom is limited still further.

In the less important things in life you may find you have more choice. You can choose within certain limits what you will do tomorrow or next weekend; whether you will attend today's lecture or sleep; how you will spend what money, if any, that remains after essentials have been paid for. But if this is the sort of freedom you are fighting for, you might possibly ask yourself just how much it is worth.

If you examine this a little more closely still, you may notice a very interesting point about your life. Your freedom allows you to fall into bad habits but very seldom into good ones. When you find yourself protesting that you are free to do what you want, the 'what you want' is almost invariably what you suspect you should not. If you doubt this, experiment for a while with being free to do good, to break all your bad habits and to live for other people. I wonder how far you will get! Certainly it looks as if we are much more free to

71

go downwards than to go upwards – as if our freedom is seriously restricted in the moral as well as in the physical sense. You may, of course, question whether the words 'good' and 'bad' have any valid meaning when it comes to choices in behaviour, but I am assuming it to be self-evident that a life of self-giving which brings health, happiness and well-being both to yourself and to others is a better life than one which, through selfishness and foolishness, brings misery and failure all round.

However reluctant we may be to admit it, human nature is such that we find it easier to do wrong than to do right. St Paul once looked at himself and described the symptoms like this : 'I do not understand my own actions. For I do not do what I want, but I do the very thing I hate ... I can will what is right, but I cannot do it ... So I find it to be a law that when I want to do right, evil lies close at hand ...'[1] If we are honest with ourselves, we must agree that this is a remarkably accurate analysis. I am not concerned to argue here whether mankind is on the up or the downgrade. What interests me is whether you are free or whether you are a slave. An investigation seems to make it plain beyond all doubt that you are not really free at all, and that in the limited field in which you can choose, your actual choices have a distinct tendency to lead you into a self-centred way of living which, at heart, you know to be wrong. What is more, this tendency proves to be irreversible. Everyone knows from personal experience that temptation acts like a drug; each time you give in it becomes progressively harder

---

[1] Romans 7:15, 18, 21.

to resist, until eventually it becomes totally dominating. It is a trap from which there is no escape if you walk in too far.

But words like 'dominating' and 'trap' suggest the very opposite of 'freedom'. In fact, a very subtle change has occurred, which can even pass almost unnoticed. Man starts by protesting his freedom, but very soon he begins to become what amounts to a slave. He ceases to have real control over his own thoughts, desires and actions. And the louder he protests his freedom, the more trapped he becomes. He goes on saying 'I do this because I want to' long after he has ceased to have any real choice in the matter. A careful look at some of your own thoughts and habits will confirm this. The kind of freedom which begins by insisting that 'I can do what I want with my own life' seems full of promise, but proves to be a one-way road to the sad realization that 'If I am honest with myself, I am now incapable of living a really good life'. Jesus Christ once summed up the situation when he said : 'Every one who commits sin is a slave to sin', and he went on to make one of his remarkable claims : 'If the Son makes you free, you will be free indeed.'[1]

If this analysis of the situation is true, then what most people call freedom is false and cruelly misleading. But what, then, is real freedom? If we now start our investigation with *God* instead of with ourselves, an answer immediately begins to emerge. If God really exists then it is little wonder that to insist, 'I can do what I want with my own life,' leads to a wrong solution; it starts from the wrong premise. It assumes that

[1] John 8:34, 36.

man is a totally independent being who exists simply for his own benefit. But if Jesus Christ was right in what he told us about God, then this is very far from being true.

Christianity states that God created you. Furthermore, he did not do it in the least haphazardly, because it is not possible for God to do anything which is not perfect in itself. This means that he created you because he wants you to fulfil a certain purpose. You have a certain part to play in the world which no-one else can play, and for this part he has given you certain abilities and talents, temperament and interests. He has, in others words, a perfect plan for your life which exactly suits you, and in the fulfilment of which you will be absolutely happy and satisfied.

It is rather like a master engineer who makes an intricate part for a machine. This part will fit only in one place, and without it the whole machine cannot function properly. But because this vast machine works by love and responsive self-giving, each part has free will. This means it can refuse to fit. It can wander all over the machine, getting in the way, and causing all kinds of damage both to itself and to the other parts. It does this on the pretext that it is free to do what it likes. But is not the truth of the matter that it is only really free, and only really of any use, when it is fitted in the right place and helping to drive the machine? It is then free to play its full part properly, and the result is both satisfaction and efficiency, as we saw in the last chapter. It seems that the use of 'freedom' to go beyond the intention of the master engineer must be self-defeating.

The truth of this is clearly illustrated in a different way in one of the most famous stories ever told : that of

74

the prodigal son.[1] God gave us life and he gave us our inheritance in the form of talents and opportunities. If we had used them in his way and according to his plan we should have been perfectly happy and satisfied. But years ago we decided that we did not want to live at home with our heavenly Father, and so we took our inheritance and walked out on God. We went to live in the far country of independence, perhaps uncomfortably aware at times that God was still longing and grieving for us, because it is impossible that such a father should cease to love his child even though he is not at all prepared to take the step of returning home. Perhaps we have sent him a post-card from time to time, and he has tried to help us when we have allowed it. Almost certainly we have sent off a telegram marked 'Urgent' when things have become too difficult. But we have not been willing to give up our so-called independence.

But as the story progressed, the son discovered to his cost that he was not really independent at all. He may have been free of his father, although love exercised a hold even at that distance, but he was in slavery to nearly everything else. Certain habits and ways of life were soon exercising an effective control over his life, and in a very practical way he became utterly dependent on money and friends. Far from becoming truly free, all he had done was to exchange dependence on his father (who would never have let him down) for dependence on friends (who did just that), money (which ran out), and habits which soon effectively neutralized his inheritance of talent. In the end he was left with

[1] Read it for yourself in Luke 15:11–32.

nothing except his own frustration, and it is clear from the story that he would have died in the far country if he had not 'come to himself' and decided to go home. 'I will arise and go to my father, and I will say to him, "Father, I have sinned against heaven and before you; I am no longer worthy to be called your son; treat me as one of your hired servants." '

The meeting which resulted between father and son is one of the most moving episodes in all literature. 'While he was yet at a distance, his father saw him and had compassion, and ran and embraced him and kissed him. And the son said to him, "Father, I have sinned against heaven and before you; I am no longer worthy to be called your son." But the father said to his servants, "Bring quickly the best robe, and put it on him; and put a ring on his hand, and shoes on his feet; and bring the fatted calf and kill it, and let us eat and make merry; for this my son was dead, and is alive again; he was lost, and is found." '

He offered to become a slave, but his father took him and made him a son. At last he was free to live the life for which he had always been intended. At last he could discover the meaning of true freedom. A strange paradox had taken place. He thought he was free, when in reality he was a slave. He surrendered his free will, thinking this would make him a slave, and it led, instead, to real freedom. The story illustrates the way back which every one of us must take for ourselves if we are to experience God's kind of freedom.

But because this vital act of self-surrender requires both faith and courage, many, many people will never take it. They will cling to their shreds of independence and indulgence like a child who will not surrender a poor, broken toy. Perhaps they will claim the doubtful privilege of being successful rebels to the end. God will not compel us to surrender. He wants to make us sons, not slaves. You cannot make anyone free by force.

When all is said and done, it depends on what kind of a God you believe in. If you think that God is going to try to do you out of something, with most enjoyable things strictly forbidden, then of course you will not feel inclined to risk his kind of freedom. But do you really believe that God is like that? If God is anything like what Jesus Christ told us – and what, indeed, centuries of Christians have experienced him to be – then there is no need for hesitation. God knows all about you from the beginning to the end. He created you and has a wonderful, exciting and perfect plan for your life. He loves you and wants the very highest and the very best for you. He is able to give you all the things you really need. He guarantees you a full, complete and successful life. Will you trust him with your life? He has made wonderful promises to those who will. Begin to read carefully through the New Testament and you will soon start to discover them for yourself. Do you believe that God will keep his promises? All those who do place the full weight of their faith in God and the promises he has made, by surrendering their life into his hands, discover for themselves that his service is perfect freedom.

9 Success

It would be surprising, and even perhaps unnatural, if the question of success were not very much in our minds. Everyone wants to be successful in one way or another. We want to be successful in our exams and in our careers; we want tremendously to be successful and popular as people; we want to be successful eventually as a husband or wife and as a parent.

It should follow logically from this that we ought to be only too willing to seek and accept advice and help from every possible source. And indeed where questions of technique or plain fact are concerned, we are usually willing to humble our pride sufficiently to do this; we consult the textbook or go to the tutor. But it is one of those strange facets of human nature that in almost any other aspect of life, the opposite tends to be true. The keener we are to be successful, the more resolutely we turn our back on other people's help and good advice. When God comes into the picture, we see this attitude very clearly. It is very often just because we are so keen to be successful that we try so hard to keep God out of our lives. We somehow have the impression that he is going to cramp our style. We want and intend to make money and we fear he may have other ideas. We want to find an attractive girl or a handsome man and we fear he may stand in our way. We want to be popular and we fear that he may want us to be 'good' in a way which will make us objects of scorn and pity.

Of course, when you set it out like this, it is easy to see that this is not in the least logical or even likely. It assumes that God is either a heavenly grandfather who wants to hand out Victorian advice, or else a super-policeman who is interested only in spoiling other people's fun. If you seriously think that God is remotely like either of these two characters, then you have not even begun to understand what Christianity is all about.[1]

Probably it is not quite as explicit in your mind as this. You just have a vague fear that God will want to interfere in your plans, and that, perhaps, is what stops you seriously considering Christianity. You do not want any interference. You are frightened for your own independence, as we saw in the previous chapter. You do not want to get too involved. But if the main argument of the last chapter is true, then there *is* only one way to success in life, and that is God's way; and there is only one way to certain and ultimate failure, and that is your way.

Of course, God's success may not look at first sight like the world's success. If you become a Christian, I cannot guarantee that you will make a fortune, although you may. I cannot even guarantee that you will

[1] See J. B. Phillips, *Your God is Too Small* (Wyvern Books).

find a husband or a wife. What I can guarantee is that you will have the peace and freedom we have already discussed, and that at the end of your life you will know that God has been with you, and has guided you according to his own plan, which is perfect and wonderful and satisfying. We all crave for satisfaction in life; God guarantees it. Christ said: 'Whoever drinks of the water that I shall give him will never thirst; the water that I shall give him will become in him a spring of water welling up to eternal life.'[1]

In the same way, when I say that without God you will fail, I am not saying that it will necessarily look like failure at first sight – although only too often and tragically that is just what it does look like. You may make a lot of money, and you may have a very happy marriage, although the number of people who succeed in doing either is surprisingly small; you may be the exception. No; real failure is to live without ever discovering what life is really all about – like playing with the pieces of a jig-saw without ever making a picture. Real failure is to feed on things which do not satisfy, to live on things which give such immediate excitement and interest that you do not realize until too late that there is nothing but emptiness underneath. Real failure is to think that you have everything that matters – only to find in the end that you have nothing that matters.

If there really is a God who made you, then true success can follow only from placing yourself entirely in his hands. He is the one who holds the key to your life. Of course, if you do this, you will not know in advance exactly what he will ask you to do. You might

[1] John 4:14.

find yourself, to your surprise, working as a missionary in a remote corner of the world; you might equally well find yourself among the thousands of Christian teachers, lawyers, doctors, or businessmen and women. God needs Christians in every job and profession in every part of the world. He has a place for you which will be both exciting and rewarding, a job which, in his plan, only you can do. What a wonderful thing it is when you can be sure as you choose your career that you are finding the place which God has chosen for you, the place which will make the very most out of your life.

Those who do believe in God and ask for his guidance in this way at important stages in their lives fall into two main groups. The first group pray for guidance and genuinely ask God to make clear what he wants. But they definitely, if sub-consciously, reserve the right to veto his decision if they think he is giving either a wrong answer, or an answer which does not fit their own ideas on the subject. The second group are prepared to believe that God knows what he is doing, and that he knows them better than they know themselves. Hence they put themselves unreservedly into his hands. It is the second group who are on the road to experiencing God's success in their lives. There is a line of a hymn which runs :

> *'Those who trust Him wholly,*
> *Find Him wholly true.'*

To make up one's mind over a matter such as one's career is to find all the theory we have been discussing suddenly coming down to earth with a bang. When it comes to an actual decision, what are you going to do?

Will you trust God and genuinely seek his guidance, putting yourself into his hands, or not? It is easy to talk vaguely about having a purpose in life; but are you prepared to live it out in practice? It is easy to say you believe in God; but are you prepared to act on your belief? It is easy to talk of love as the supreme virtue; but are you prepared to live as if it were true?

The choice of a career is, of course, the beginning rather than the end of the problem of success. Supposing that we do believe that God has created every one of us with a particular role in mind,[1] and that only in this can we experience true success; supposing that we believe, furthermore, that God will show us what that role is if we will let him. There remains the problem of actually living it out 'successfully'. Does God expect us to make a success of his calling on our own? Fortunately he does not. If the first secret of success in life is to follow his guidance, the second is to experience his power.

We are all tempted to think we do not need it – until we get involved in a situation we cannot handle. So we find ourselves using God as a sort of fire escape – for use only in emergencies, even if we do this a little shamefacedly. But God is very good to us even here, and you will remember that the prodigal son received a wonderful welcome, in spite of the fact that he would probably never have come home at all if the situation had not become desperate.

If we are honest with ourselves, we probably know

[1] I use the general word 'role' here because God's plan for your life may well include more than one 'job' or 'profession'. It may include many over the course of a lifetime.

at heart that we need God's help and strength every day of our lives – and the incredible fact is that we can have it for the asking. And if we live in God's strength, then how can we fail in life? It is impossible. St Paul once realized in triumph that 'I can do *all things* in him who strengthens me'.[1] Nothing is impossible for a man if God is with him. His prospects in life are unlimited.

[1] Philippians 4:13.

10 Service

There is one other important area of discussion which we must look at briefly before seeking to pull the various loose ends together. The thoughtful reader may well be wondering by now whether much of the discussion so far has not been too dominated by self-interest. We have been concerned with our own personal purpose and value, freedom and success. We have looked carefully at our own personal relationship with God, and asked whether we are self-centred or God-centred.

But surely there is another aspect to this altogether; should we not also be 'neighbour-centred'? If the first commandment is 'You shall love the Lord your God with all your heart, and with all your soul, and with all your mind,' then is not the second 'You shall love your neighbour as yourself'?[1] Ought we not, in other words, to be living for other people rather than for ourselves? Many people today are less worried about questions of their own salvation and even success, than

[1] Matthew 22:37, 39.

they are about their neighbour's welfare. It is the lack of social justice and peace, the existence of famine and oppression and nuclear weapons which really concern them. What is more, it is precisely here that they feel Christianity has failed to provide an adequate answer.

The first essential at this point is to beware of a confusion of thought. Interest today in 'social' issues does not spring from an interest in 'society' as such; it springs from an interest in the individual. We live, in fact, in an age of individualism. For better or for worse, the established social 'units' of society – the family, the village, the church and the state – are being progressively broken down. Even the units of nation, race and colour are disintegrating before our eyes. Man has become conscious of himself as an individual as perhaps never before.[1]

The effect of this is twofold. First, man has become conscious of his own destiny in a new way. He thinks of himself as an individual, carefully differentiated from the society in which he lives. The dangers of this are obvious. What happens when the aims and progress of the society run foul of the successful progress and self-expression of the individual? Individualism can easily result in a deadly competition which sets everyone, consciously or unconsciously, against his neighbour. But at the very least it makes everyone *aware* of his neighbour. Thus, if the first effect of individualism is to make a man conscious of himself, the

[1] Communism is, of course, the main representative in the modern world of the opposite viewpoint, the subjugation of the individual to the larger unit of the state. This is one main reason for the head-on ideological clash between East and West.

second is to make him conscious of other people as individuals.

Hence our 'social' concern today; if we are more concerned about the problem of food shortage in India or refugees in Asia than we were a hundred years ago, this is due in large measure to the fact that we can now see an Indian peasant or an Asian child as an individual, with the same hopes and fears, the same needs and the same rights as ourselves. In the same way we see problems of war, slavery and cruelty in a very different light from our ancestors. The practical effects of this outlook can hardly be overestimated, and it lies at the root of the great social revolution of our time.

My defence, therefore, for concentrating attention so far on the individual is quite simply that it is the individual who is important. What we should now be beginning to see is that this is not the whole story. If it is logical, in an age such as ours, to *begin* our investigation with the individual, it would nevertheless be fatal to leave the impression on anyone's mind that the matter *ends* there.

What we must now do is to come back yet once more to the question of the existence and character of God, and see if we cannot catch something of the Christian vision of the world. If it is true that God loves *you* and has a perfect plan and purpose for your life, then this must also be true of every other person in this world, whether that person be black or white, Western or Eastern, primitive or cultured, rich or poor. If God created you, then he also created each one of them; if he can make your life truly successful, then he can do the same with their lives also. There is nothing in this book which applies to you which does not apply in just the same way to every other inhabitant of this earth. Before God all men are equal.

Let us then suppose for a moment that you decide to become a Christian, and give your life over into God's hands where it belongs. You will then find not only the salvation which comes from a right relationship with God, but also that God can now control your life to give you the true freedom and success we have already discussed. But it follows from what we have just seen about God that his plan for your life will lead you inevitably into a right relationship of love and service for other people. If God loves your neighbour as much as he loves you, then clearly his will for your life will lead you to give expression to the commandment to love your neighbour as yourself. In the same way, of course, if your neighbour becomes a Christian, he will find himself led to love and serve you, as well as all his other neighbours.

The individual approach thus turns out to be not even remotely selfish and results in an entirely new attitude to other people, each of whom is a child of God. 'Saved to serve,' a motto of the Salvation Army, sums up the situation exactly. God does not seek us out just for our own benefit at all, but so that we may be used by him to help forward his purpose of redeeming the world.

You may possibly be wondering why it is that a book on Christianity has so far made hardly even a passing reference to the 'church'. But it is only now, as we take this argument one step further, that we can begin to see where the church fits into the picture. If we stand back and look at the world in relationship to God, we can see that his concern is not ultimately with a collection of isolated individuals; he is concerned with a new world society – a new heaven and a new earth, peopled by men and women living in responsive love and self-giving both to God and to each other. This is the world as God intended it to be, and although man's abuse of his free will has produced a hideously different picture, God's intention cannot in the end be frustrated. In other words, the Christian believes he is on the winning side. 'If God is for us, who is against us?'[1]

Such a vision pertains partly to a new age. It will be the work of God and lies still in the future. But it pertains also to the present, because wherever there is a man or woman in the world doing God's will under his direction, then there is a living sign of the new age and a living means whereby it will be brought about. God works through ordinary individuals like you and me to achieve his final purpose for the world.

How many people can he count on in the world today? However discredited Christianity may seem in some quarters, the answer nevertheless lies in millions. In virtually every corner of the earth you will find men and women from every nation, of every colour, class and language, quietly dedicated to God and to the fulfilment of his will for the world. This is God's church, his task force on earth. Every Christian is a member of his church, related to each other in a special way. This is because they are already fellow-citizens of the new age, living in trust and obedience to God and in love for one another, and their task is to bring about a new society, in which all the evils and problems which beset us today can no longer exist. And because God is with

[1] Romans 8:31.

them, success is assured in the end, although it will come in his time and in his way.

This is, the Christian believes, to see the world and its history in true perspective. It is not a question of fighting a lone battle in life either for the sake of self-interest and worldly success, or for the sake of other people and social justice and peace. Much more is at stake. It is a question of giving one's allegiance to the cause of the devil or to the cause of God. It is a question of whose side you are on.

The church as we see it, of course, does not always look like God's task force on earth, nor does it always seem to be on the winning side. Christians are not always worthy of the God they worship, and no-one would pretend they are. The incredible fact is that God is willing to accept and to be identified with very fallible human beings. He guides, helps and uses us in every way in which we will let him, but he does not entirely overrule in all our mistakes and foolishness, or no doubt we would cease to be human. God's church is a living witness to the fact that there is no-one whom God will not accept and use.

Today, in a world which has come close to turning its back on him altogether, God needs dedicated men and women, who will humbly be prepared to be part of his 'task force', not more ashamed than he is of his church, who will serve him better than those whom they feel inclined to criticize. Will you be one of them? To become a Christian is to be a member of a redeemed society, set on winning the world back to God, in his power and with his love. It is in this way, and in this way only, that peace and prosperity can become the birthright of every individual in every part of the world.

God has no other way than through the reconciling love and sacrifice of Jesus Christ, and he has no other means than ordinary people like you and me.

11 Action

I wonder what you will do when you have finished reading this book! The immediate answer will probably be 'Go and have tea' or perhaps 'Go to sleep'; but what do you propose to do next about Christianity? Unless you are utterly convinced that there is nothing in it at all, God at least requires the courtesy of further investigation. The New Testament evidence is there for all to read. There are suggestions for further reading at the end of this chapter; you are probably within reach of a Christian friend, a church or a Christian Union, and they would always welcome an investigator, provided you come with an open mind; you might even use the subjects of these chapters as the bases for discussions.

There are many possibilities. What is important to realize at this stage is that your life is going to be vitally affected if you reach the conclusion that God really exists and that he really loves you. This is not merely an academic question to be argued about over coffee, nor is it going to help you much in the long run to be able to produce semi-philosophical arguments either for or against. There is nothing easier than to shelve the whole matter if you really want to – after all, most people do; but this is not a satisfactory solution to the problem. Indeed it is not a solution at all, and there is nothing remotely clever about it. It is much better to have the courage to face the evidence for Christianity honestly and squarely and be prepared to follow wherever it may lead.

Your decision is important. Your life is before you – what are you going to do with it? Today, as in every age, there are many gods and creeds calling for your consideration, and whether you like it or not, you are bound to end up by giving your allegiance to one of them. Most people in the West nowadays find themselves worshipping the god of materialism – Follow me and I will turn you into the sort of person you see on all the advertisements: rich, successful and compellingly attractive. Is this promise fulfilled in most cases? Are these the right aims in life anyway? Is this a false god drawing its adherents into ultimate disillusionment? The God revealed to us in Jesus Christ makes different, but no less far-reaching promises: 'I am the light of the world; he who follows me will not walk in darkness, but will have the light of life.'[1] 'I am the bread of life; he who comes to me shall not hunger, and he who believes in me shall never thirst.'[2] 'I am the way, and the truth, and the life.'[3]

It may well be that you have never thought of Christianity before as being particularly important. Perhaps you know a person who claims to be a

[1] John 8:12.   [2] John 6:35.   [3] John 14:6.

Christian, but his faith does not seem to have the slightest effect on his life. Whether this charge is true or false, it gives the impression that Christianity is not really relevant to life. But clearly a faith that makes no difference to a person's life is not really a faith at all. That person might as well give up his belief for all the good it is doing him. The apostle Paul had some very hard words to say once about people who have a form of godliness but deny the power of it. I am assuming that if you do believe in God and decide to follow Jesus Christ, he will become the centre point of your life around which all else revolves. If God exists at all, he is important enough for that.

Having grasped the importance of what is at stake, the second stage is carefully to examine the evidence. I have tried to give a very brief introduction to the Christian faith. It claims that Jesus Christ came to show us what God is like, both by the life he lived and by his death and resurrection. He showed us that God, the creator of all things, loves us just as we are and whatever we may have done. He showed us on the cross the power of that love and the lengths to which love would go to win us back out of that 'far country'. He showed us the love which can heal, restore and forgive, and which can take our lives and make them new and whole. He showed us the love that longs and pleads for the response of faith in our hearts and lives.

The evidence is there for you to examine. There can be no reason for anyone to say he did not know. Jesus Christ lived in the full light of history. What he did, what he said and what he claimed are there for all to read and judge. The evidence of those who followed him and were eye-witnesses of the events has been written down for our benefit. The evidence of Christians all down the centuries is likewise there for examination, and indeed the evidence of Christians among your own friends and neighbours is available also. The facts are all around; how do you interpet them?

If you do examine this evidence for yourself and find it convincing, then what does God require of you? What do you have to do? Do you have to give up everything you possess? Must you begin to live a life of perfect goodness and love immediately? Fortunately that is not what God asks of us. He asks something which is, by comparison, drastically simple, although in another way terribly hard. He asks us simply to turn to him in repentance and faith, seeking his forgiveness for our sin and placing our lives under his care. This is the response he seeks to his love and all that he has done for us. I wonder if you are prepared for that.

If you are, you can be sure you will never be disappointed. It is not possible that God will let you down. What is more, you will begin at last to understand what life is all about. You will experience for yourself the gradual unfolding of his wonderful plan for your life. You will experience for yourself the power and love of God as you actually begin to live out that plan. You will begin to live the life you were created for. It will be the beginning of a life which will suddenly take on unlimited prospects and unlimited hope. Certainly there is not the least possibility that it will be dull. It stands to reason that life with God will be the most exciting and at the same time most satisfying life that there is. You will begin to learn about purpose and value, about love and faith, about peace, freedom and success.

To become a Christian, then, requires a definite step of faith. It is rather like risking your life by stepping on to a bridge over a gorge. First of all, you examine, if you are wise, the construction and the foundations of that bridge. These are the facts. You must interpret them and judge whether the bridge seems solid. But this is not enough on its own. You must then trust your judgment, exercise faith, and step on to the bridge. Carefully at first, but with increasing confidence, you will walk out and find the structure firm beneath your feet. You never will know the real strength of the bridge until you walk on it. You never will know for certain whether God is real or not until you put yourself in a position in which you depend on him, until you place yourself in a situation from which you cannot retreat. This is what faith means, and God demands faith from every one of us.

God has given us a free will, and he expects us to use it. We can stay on the bank if we wish, or we can spend our lives talking about the foundations. But it is those who make the venture of faith, and, at the risk of making fools of themselves – yes, at the risk of falling into the river – begin to walk, who discover in their own experience that God is the rewarder of those who seek him with all their hearts, and who put their trust in him completely.

SUGGESTIONS FOR FURTHER READING

Basic Christianity, John R. W. Stott (IVP).
Mere Christianity, C. S. Lewis (Fontana).
Christian Beliefs, I. H. Marshall (IVP).
Your God is Too Small, J. B. Phillips (Wyvern Books).
Christian Doctrine, J. S. Whale (Fontana).
Choose Freedom, Michael Green (IVP).
Why I am a Christian, O. Hallesby (IVP).
Christian Faith Today, Stephen Neill (Pelican Books).
The Man from Outside, Gordon Bridger (IVP).
The Living God, R. T. France (IVP).
My God is Real, David Watson (Falcon).